About the Author

The author of this poetry, Marianna Dobis, probably even now as you read this, cannot believe she, at the age of twenty-one, published her first book. She is a dreamer who always decides by heart, but when it comes to the final decision still tends to need a "push" from the ones she loves. She was born in a small town in Slovakia where she lived until she moved to England in 2021.

The Things I Have Never Told You

Marianna Dobis

The Things I Have Never Told You

Olympia Publishers
London

www.olympiapublishers.com
OLYMPIA PAPERBACK EDITION

A CIP catalogue record for this title is
available from the British Library.

ISBN: 978-1-80074-862-0

This is a work of fiction.
Names, characters, places and incidents originate from the writer's
imagination. Any resemblance to actual persons, living or dead, is
purely coincidental.

First Published in 2022

Olympia Publishers
Tallis House
2 Tallis Street
London
EC4Y 0AB

Printed in Great Britain

Dedication

For all the lonely souls out there that believe, there is something more... There actually really is, just keep searching for it, my dear.

Dedicated to my beloved parents, Eva and Jozef. All I have, I have thanks to you. No matter where I am, a part of me is still with you.
I love you.
—Your daughter

Acknowledgements

A huge "Thank you" to all the people who believed in me. I have done it just because you thought I could.

My honest confession,
because I cannot keep it to myself any more.

In you I found my inspiration
in you I found my poetry
in you I found me

It's all good…
sometimes

I promise you
that he felt
quite like a miracle

How come these things that are the hardest to tell
be also the most important to let know?

You are everything but basic

Just get yourself ready for all the miracles
'cause they are about to come
sooner than you think

And at least we still look at the same stars at night

I assume that forgetting
would give me both
freedom and emptiness

Don't fight with it,
it happened for a reason

I hope you know
that you live with me every day
for you live in me every day

You are so scared to feel something
that it scares me in the first place

All of us are broken,
it's just about finding somebody
who will love you a little bit more
when all that hurt comes out from time to time

And since I know him
I don't need any other evidence
that there is pure magic in this world

I just want to treasure
all these moments
in me forever.
And I will,
I know I will

And since I met you
I had no need to search for my
once in a lifetime person any more

I don't know why,
but somehow
it's still you

And the moment when I realised
I care about you so much
that you could break my heart one day
was also the moment
when I promised myself
I will never let you do so

I just hope to see you again
but not only in my dreams
where I meet you daily

Every new day brings me something beautiful
and every "something beautiful" makes me think of you.
So yes, I guess that's the reason why I cannot get you out of
my mind

I can tell you everything I know about him,
I can tell you what I saw in those eyes,
I can tell you what he felt like when he touched me,
I can tell you how he made me feel.
But please, do not ask me why it could only be him,
because I don't know either

If there is something that I have learned
about love in my early twenties
it is that love really can be anything
but forced

Search and you will find
that special kind of love,
not only a chemistry
because chemistry without love
is just as useless as
love without chemistry

You really are one of a kind…
you always will be,
so please remember that

And eventually
he will save himself
because that's just what he does

When I saw you
that day I promised myself
that you must be the reason
why the sun decides to shine every new day
I think that I could shine for you every day too

These beautiful, old memories
I have with you
start to fade away day by day.
I think I am ready
for new ones, darling

It was strange you know...
he read me like an open book
and found those pieces in me
I never thought even existed

Even though it wasn't a love story
it surely could be one

And then there was you
right in the middle of all the chaos
as the only thing that has given me some sense ever
and plenty of hope too

Last night,
I was mulling
about you once again…
and I found myself thinking
if I die not knowing
what it feels like
to be kissed by you

So now I just live my life
trying to reconcile
with a fact
that I will simply
never forget you

I simply don't believe
that there is anyone in this world
who deserves
to be loved by you

You and I,
we were the best definition of
so close and yet so far

On days like this
I just wish a little bit more
you would be here
holding my hand

Maybe it was short
but it was for sure real
and that is enough for me
in order to remember it forever

There is no need for me
to watch these love stories on TV any more
for I have experienced something similar
but real and stronger

Don't worry,
I didn't fall in love with you
but I know I surely did fall for that feeling
that no one else could give me but you

And if there was a person
in this world
who could save me
it would surely be you

I saw you and
I could imagine
waking up next to you
for the rest of my life
if that ain't magic,
then there is none in this world

I don't believe in perfection
but I do believe in you
and that's basically the same thing

You have no idea
how much you mean to me
and that's probably good

Forget all these "special" moments my dear,
for they have been seen as something special
only for you, not for him

I thought that by writing it would be easier to forget about you
but I can feel that it has the exact opposite effect
'cause when I write about you
I think about the moments we had
I think about us
what gives me conviction
that there was some "us" once,
even though I know it wasn't

Sometimes I find myself
thinking that it's not over yet
that it couldn't be.
Because if it is, then why all of that?
I mean, this feeling was too strong to be useless

And how would I describe it in general?
I think one cannot really understand
if he hadn't felt it.
But I would probably just say that
some things cannot be forced
just the same way as
some others cannot be denied

I don't want to tell them
what is so special about you
because I fear they would fall for you too
even though I cannot understand
how they haven't noticed by themselves yet

It's okay by me
that we were not meant to be
'cause at least we still were meant to meet
and have our moments together
and for me that was more than enough

I tried, I really did, I tried so hard
but I cannot stop it now
so I just try to cope with living
an ordinary life with
extraordinary memories

Sometimes I just don't understand
how could this all even happen.
Like how can one particular person be so important to you
and give a whole new dimension to your world
and how much that particular person can give you
only because of his existence.
I just don't get it; it's quite like a strange disease, isn't it?

As I met him,
I wished I had a chance
to be a part of his life much earlier
just the same as I wished
I will never stop to be
from then on

I still don't know what it was
but I can for sure tell you
that it was a lot stronger than me

The sooner you understand
that there is nobody who can ever make you feel like him
the sooner you can carry on living like it never happened
because that's what you have to do,
you have to carry on,
you mustn't get yourself stuck
in that moment forever

I am not perfect
and you are not perfect as well
but together we could be so close
to perfection like never before

And even though you are
hundreds of miles away from me
I still feel you much closer
than the person
sitting in the same room with me

I just hope that someday
there will be somebody
who will look at me
and think the same things
that I think of
when looking at you

Even a thought about losing you
hurts like hell
and I don't really get it
because I never really had you
in the first place

And suddenly
I understand life
so much more
since you are a part of mine

I just wanted to let you know that
in you I found all the inspiration
I would ever need
and for that
I will be forever grateful no matter what

It's okay darling,
you do not have to be sorry for feeling it
it happened for a reason,
and even though it has no continuation
it still was real
and nothing wrong,
nothing to be sorry for

No matter where I am or what I do
a part of me is somehow still with you

And what now?

What will happen next?

Will I ever meet somebody who will feel like home again?

Will he feel that I could be his home too?

And most importantly, will he stay?

Or will he give up before he even starts just the same as you?

I know that you wanted to go away
but that does not stop me from thinking
about how bad I wanted you to stay

I had no idea I was missing something
but then you showed up
and gave me all of that

So please,
just look at me
and watch the way I stay

I have given up hoping
that I will find you someday
but then you came

Just in case you have been wondering
nothing changed.
It's still you today
just the same way
how it still was you yesterday
and will be you tomorrow

Maybe it's not about the happy ending
maybe it just simply cannot really end

I am all alone,
but I am still with him at the same time
in fact, I don't think he can ever be gone
even though he is so far away from me

We all have one particular story
we don't talk about
and somehow
you are mine

It felt like an explosion in me
and I had no idea
what to do with that at all
so I just played with my hair
trying to stay calm and
hoping he wouldn't notice a thing
of course he noticed

I still look for you
in every new person I meet

Before I met you I had always thought that
the hardest part will be meeting
somebody so special.
But now as I know you
I understand that it's actually
the way you hold me and don't
at the same time

It was way too much
but somehow
still not enough

Some stories are way too private
to be told out loud

The hardest part was trying to stay calm
when my whole world was shaking
as I became lost in your eyes
I tried so hard so you wouldn't notice a thing
but it took me just a quick look at your smile
and I knew I failed

And I still cannot find the words
that could describe how I felt
in fact, I have never known
that a person can feel so much
in just one moment

Sometimes I really feel I had enough
of thinking about you
so I just go to sleep
to stop it at least for a while
but then you suddenly appear
in every nice dream I have
as a reminder that
you are never gone,
that you cannot be

We found each other a long time ago
I think it just took us a while
to understand that it's real

The fact that I could sleep
so peacefully next to him
scared me like nothing before

You were more than enough for me
and I was more than enough for you.
Who could have known
that more than enough
can also not be enough?

And if I'm not the one for you,
will you at least remember me?

And if you find yourself
in these words as well,
please let me know.
Because I need to know
I'm not the only one here
losing my mind.